DROUGHT

DROUGHT

CHRISTOPHER LAMPTON

THE MILLBROOK PRESS
BROOKFIELD, CT
A DISASTER! BOOK

Illustrations by Pat Scully
Photographs courtesy of Superstock: cover, pp. 6, 11, 30, 37, 45; United
Nations: pp. 8–9, 24, 25, 26, 27; Photo Researchers: pp. 12–13 (© Joseph
Nettis), 23 (© Frank Schreiber), 48 (© A. W. Ambler), 52 (© Lawrence Migdale),
54 (© Farrell Grehan); United States Department of Agriculture: pp. 15, 43;
Library of Congress: pp. 16, 17, 18–19; Magnum Photos, © Philip J. Griffiths:
pp. 20, 42–43; National Archives: p. 21; National Weather Service: p. 39;
National Optical Astronomy Observatories: p. 49.

Library of Congress Cataloging-in-Publication Data
Lampton, Christopher.
Drought / by Christopher Lampton.
p.   cm.—(A Disaster! book)
Includes bibliographical references and index.
Summary: Investigates the causes and disastrous effects of drought, giving the his-
tory of some of the severest droughts on record in the United States and elsewhere.
ISBN 1-878841-91-2 (pbk.)
1. Droughts—Juvenile literature. [1. Droughts.] I. Title. II. Series.
QC929.D8L28 1992   91-18053
551.57'73—dc20   CIP   AC

123456789 - WO - 96 95 94 93 92

CONTENTS

WORLD WITHOUT RAIN

You never noticed when the rains stopped coming. Maybe that's because the weather was so beautiful. At first, you were delighted when you stepped out of your house every day to find blue skies and fair weather. You began to plan picnics and visits to the beach. You were glad that it didn't rain anymore because rain got in the way of all the things you wanted to do.

In a drought, the rains usually don't stop altogether. It just doesn't rain enough to be of any use to people or crops.

7

Or maybe you didn't notice that it had stopped raining because it never really *did* stop. It still rained occasionally, just not as often as it used to. There would sometimes be a quick cloudburst in the late afternoon. But it was so brief and the rainwater dried up so quickly afterward that you hardly noticed it.

After a while, though, you began to notice certain changes taking place. The grass in your yard began to turn brown. The flowers in the garden needed to be watered more often. Exposed patches of dirt began to dry up. Cracks started to run across the surface of the ground.

Then you heard the announcements on the radio. They said that you shouldn't wash your car anymore or water your garden. And before long, local authorities were asking you to bathe less often and to drink less tap water.

Finally, water rationing began. The government announced that everybody would be allowed to use only a certain small amount of water a day. Anyone who used more would be fined. People caught washing their car would be subject to a jail sentence. There was even a limit on the number of times a day that you could flush your toilet.

But that wasn't the worst of it. Certain foods began disappearing from the grocery store. In fact, the shelves in certain sections of the store were beginning to look positively bare. When you turned on the water faucet, only a trickle of liquid came out. And the rains came less and less often, until it seemed like they never came at all.

After weeks without watering, the plants in your garden died. Your lawn turned completely brown, with large bare spots in the middle of it. And then dark clouds began to appear in the sky, dark clouds that didn't carry rain with them. They were clouds of dust, blowing out of a dust-filled landscape where grass used to grow. Sometimes these clouds of dust would grow so thick that you couldn't see out of the window of your house. And you didn't dare to leave your home, because the minute you did your eyes, nose, and mouth would begin to fill with dust.

What had happened? you wondered. Why was your life suddenly turned topsy-turvy? Where had the rains gone?

What had happened was a disaster that has happened again and again in the history of the planet earth. What had happened was *drought*.

On the Sahel in Africa, droughts are common, as are dust-filled landscapes and long stretches of barren land.

WHAT IS
A DROUGHT?

A drought is a period when it rains less often than usual. It doesn't usually stop raining completely during a drought. It just doesn't rain enough to replace the water that is used or that disappears through evaporation. (We'll tell you more about evaporation in a moment.)

All living things, from plants to human beings, need water to survive. Usually, water is available in abundance. After all, it is one of the most plentiful substances on the surface of the earth. But sometimes water doesn't get to the places where it's needed at the times when it's needed—or in the form in which it's needed. Without rainfall to bring new supplies of fresh water from time to time, life on this planet might well cease to exist.

There will always be water on the planet earth, but there will always be droughts, too. In fact, there are small droughts somewhere on this planet every year. You've probably been through a

All living things need water to survive.

few of them yourself. Maybe the grass on your lawn or in parks in your neighborhood began to turn brown. Or the local authorities announced that water would be rationed and asked you not to wash your car or water your garden.

Usually, such small droughts are short and not terribly harmful. They tend to happen in the summer, when the weather is hot and dry. But sometimes droughts get out of hand. They can go on for months or even years. In a few cases they can last for as long as a decade. (Sometimes they can go on for thousands of years, but

then we don't call them droughts. Rather, we say that the area that doesn't get rain has a naturally dry *climate*. Climate is a weather pattern that lasts for long periods of time.)

The worst drought in American history took place in the twentieth century. Many people still living today remember it. It swept across the Great Plains states, including Texas, Oklahoma, Nebraska, and Kansas.

The drought lasted for almost the entire decade of the 1930s. It changed the lives of millions of people.

In a mild drought, the grass on your lawn might get brown patches, and you might be asked not to wash your car.

THE DIRTY THIRTIES

The Great Plains states are sometimes known as the nation's "breadbasket," because of the many farms there that provide food for people around the country. Rugged settlers moved into this area in the late 1800s to build farms and raise families. Life in the Great Plains was not easy in the beginning, but it paid off. The soil of the area was rich, and the farms that were established by these settlers became large and fruitful.

Then, in the 1930s, drought arrived. After fifteen years of abundant rainfall, the rain stopped coming. The year 1930 was one of

The Great Plains is the nation's "breadbasket."

the driest on record. Crops failed for lack of water. But the drought did not end that year. Although there was some rain in 1931, the drought returned in full force in 1932. And it stayed on until 1936, affecting not only the Great Plains states but much of the rest of the United States as well. And in some parts of the Great Plains, the drought lingered until the early 1940s.

This migrant family from the Dust Bowl
is heading west in search of work.

The result was terrible devastation. When the crops died, many farming families were left homeless. They began migrating westward, to the coast, where conditions were not as bad. There, these homeless families were unkindly referred to as "Okies," because many of them came from Oklahoma, one of the states hit hardest by the drought.

A hapless "Okie," his broken-down jalopy with his family and all their possessions inside, looks grimly across the desert.

This family from Arkansas is on a 900-mile trek by foot to find food and employment.

Swarms of grasshoppers, like this one, devoured the leftover crops, leaving massive starvation in their wake.

As if the drought weren't bad enough, plagues of grasshoppers and other insects began to descend on the Great Plains. They were looking for food. They ate whatever crops the drought had not taken. Rabbits also scoured the land for the last of the crops. Many of these rabbits wound up being killed for food by hungry farmers.

And then the dust storms began. As the crops and other vegetation died, they left bare earth behind. This situation was made worse by the farming practices of the late 1800s and early 1900s. Farmers had torn out the natural vegetation and planted crops instead. But it was the natural vegetation that had long protected the soil from erosion. With both the natural vegetation and the crops gone, the ground simply dried up and began to blow away in the wind.

The dust storms were known as *black blizzards* because of the way the sky turned black when they arrived. They contained millions of tons of dark soil, carried by the wind from what used to be farmlands. They blew across the plains and down the streets of cities. They covered automobiles, homes, even people with thick layers of dust. Some people got caught in the storms and choked to death on the dust; others wore gas masks to protect themselves. Cattle and other farm animals died by the thousands.

The dust storms blew as far east as New York and Massachusetts. It is from these dust storms that the decade got its nickname—the "dirty thirties." The areas of the Great Plains hit hardest with black blizzards came to be known as the "Dust Bowl."

A dust storm races toward a farming community during the drought of the 1930s. The once-fertile earth just dries up and blows away in the wind.

OTHER DROUGHTS, OTHER TIMES

The drought of the dirty thirties was very severe, but it was hardly the only drought in history—or even the worst.

The country of India has known more than its share of droughts. As we will see later, India is one of several countries that are dependent on a strong wind known as the *monsoon* for its rainstorms. When the wind doesn't blow and the rains don't come, the crops stop growing—and people begin to die.

A terrible drought struck India in the years 1769 and 1770. It was accompanied by epidemics of disease, which attacked people already weakened by starvation and dehydration (lack of water). When it was over, 10 million people had died. Drought returned to India a century later, in 1865 and 1866, killing another 10 million people.

*Monsoons rain down on a small village
in Indonesia, bringing needed moisture.*

China is also dependent on the monsoon winds for its rain. Like India, it has suffered periodically from devastating droughts. Millions of people were killed by a drought in northern China in the years 1876 through 1879. The Chinese government sent food to the starving to help relieve the suffering, but those who were to deliver the food were attacked by hungry bandits. Perhaps as many as 13 million people died over a four-year period.

In recent years, no area on earth has been more devastated by drought and famine than the continent of Africa, especially the

Sahel region. This is a narrow stretch of land that crosses much of northern Africa. Because it is a semi-dry area that borders on the Saharan desert, it is very sensitive to changes in weather patterns and can easily be pushed into a drought.

One such drought occurred in the late 1960s, and it was even worse than the droughts normally experienced by the Sahel. It lasted for the better part of a decade, ending in the mid-1970s. As many as 200,000 people died as a result of this drought. More than 30 million farm animals also died, which added to the devastation.

These scenes of the Sahel in Africa, an area particularly prone to drought, reveal a culture that has had to deal with drought and abnormally dry weather for centuries.

The land of the Sahel is not well-suited to growing food, and the droughts of the last three decades have brought great suffering and death.

In the 1980s, several other areas of Africa were struck by drought. The result was a mass *famine* (shortage of food) that lasted for much of the decade and took thousands more lives.

What causes drought? Rain is such a normal (and sometimes annoying) part of our lives that it's surprising to think that it can simply go away for long periods of time. What is it that interrupts the normal cycle of the weather and brings about a drought?

For the answer, we'll have to look at how the weather cycle works. In particular, let's look at the way in which water becomes rain—and in which rain, in turn, becomes rivers and oceans.

THE HYDROLOGIC CYCLE

If you've ever watched a river flow, you might have wondered where all of that water comes from. Rivers seem to keep flowing forever, and they almost never run out of water. Why not?

Rivers don't run out of water because they flow in a circle. You can't see the whole circle because part of it is invisible. The water in the river takes the form of *water vapor,* which can't be seen by the human eye. And instead of flowing through riverbeds, water vapor "flows" through the air itself.

There are three different forms of water. Ordinarily, water is in liquid form. This is the form that we think of when we think of water. But water also has a solid form—ice. And it has a gaseous form, which is the water vapor we just mentioned. When water is in its gaseous form, it is as invisible as the air around us. In fact, the air around us is made up, in part, of water vapor.

Water vapor enters the air whenever air and water come together. On warm days, there is more water vapor than on cold days.
Water in the ocean, for instance, can take the form of water vapor
and enter the air. So can the water in lakes, rivers, and mud pud-
dles. Even the water in your body, when it leaves your pores in the
form of perspiration, can become water vapor. When liquid water
turns into water vapor, we say that the water has *evaporated* (a
word that means "turned into vapor").

When the air near the ground rises, it carries water vapor upward with it. The higher the air rises above the ground, the colder it becomes. Cold air can't hold as much water vapor as warm air. So the water vapor *condenses*—that is, it turns back into tiny droplets of water. These droplets are so tiny that they can float in the air, forming a cloud. The next time you look up and see a cloud, you'll know that the droplets that make up the cloud were once water vapor in the air near the ground.

Eventually, the droplets of water in the cloud will clump together to form larger droplets. When the droplets become too big to float in the air, they fall back to the ground as rain. This rain fills lakes and mud puddles· and is the source of water in rivers. That's

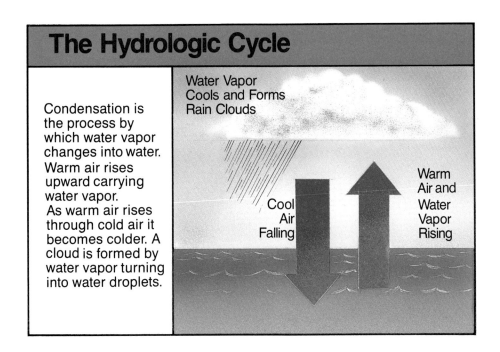

The Hydrologic Cycle

Condensation is the process by which water vapor changes into water. Warm air rises upward carrying water vapor.
As warm air rises through cold air it becomes colder. A cloud is formed by water vapor turning into water droplets.

Water Vapor Cools and Forms Rain Clouds

Cool Air Falling

Warm Air and Water Vapor Rising

why rivers never run out of water. When the water on the ground evaporates, it is returned to the river in the form of rain.

If you followed a drop of water for a few days or weeks in its life, you would find that it was always moving in a circle. First it falls as rain or snow. Then it flows down a river or sits in a lake or mud puddle or ocean. After a while, it evaporates and is carried back up into the clouds. And finally it falls back to the ground again as rain or snow.

This cycle, which has repeated itself over and over again for the billions of years that the planet earth has existed, is called the *hydrologic cycle.* It is the hydrologic cycle that keeps water continually moving around, so that rivers don't run dry and lakes don't disappear. Because all living creatures on earth need water, it is the hydrologic cycle that keeps us alive.

But the hydrologic cycle can be interrupted. That is, it may no longer continue to move water around. When this happens, the supply of water in an area can start to dry up.

The result is a drought.

THE CAUSES OF DROUGHT

Let's suppose, for instance, that water keeps evaporating but doesn't fall back to the ground as rain. As a result, the water on the ground starts to dry up without being replaced. Rivers stop flowing. Lakes go dry. Farmland becomes parched and crops die. Reservoirs—places where water is stored for piping into homes and factories—gradually empty, so that there's no water to drink.

What could cause such a thing to happen? Why would part of the hydrologic cycle stop working?

In order for water vapor to turn into rain, the air containing the water vapor must rise. But air doesn't always rise. Whether or not air rises depends on the *air pressure*.

What is air pressure? Like everything else, air has weight. It presses down on the ground just as a book presses down on a shelf or a barbell presses down on a weight lifter. This air pressure is also called *barometric pressure,* because we can measure it with a device called a *barometer.* A barometer is literally a scale for weighing the air.

When the air pressure is high—that is, when the air is heavy—it doesn't rise easily. In fact, the air actually falls. Air high in the sky gradually sinks lower and lower until it is near the ground. As a result, no water vapor is carried upward.

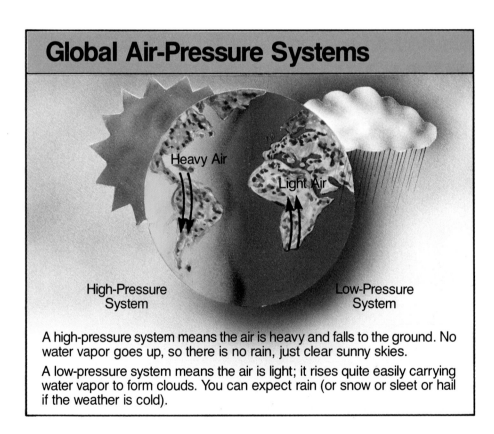

Global Air-Pressure Systems

Heavy Air

Light Air

High-Pressure System

Low-Pressure System

A high-pressure system means the air is heavy and falls to the ground. No water vapor goes up, so there is no rain, just clear sunny skies.

A low-pressure system means the air is light; it rises quite easily carrying water vapor to form clouds. You can expect rain (or snow or sleet or hail if the weather is cold).

On the other hand, when the air pressure is low—that is, when the air is light—it rises quite easily. Light air rises constantly, carrying water vapor upward with it.

When the air pressure is low, water vapor is carried upward to form clouds. These might be storm clouds. When the air pressure is high, the sky tends to be sunny and blue, with no clouds in sight.

Thus, when the weather forecaster tells you that you are in the middle of a *high-pressure system,* you can expect fair weather, with no rain or other forms of precipitation. And when the weather forecaster tells you that you are in the middle of a *low-pressure system,* you can expect rain (or snow or sleet or hail if the weather is cold).

Offhand, you'd probably prefer to be in a high-pressure system, because the weather is nicer when the air pressure is high. But the hydrologic cycle needs rain. Lakes and rivers will go dry if it doesn't rain. Crops and other plants will begin to die. And a high-pressure system can keep it from raining.

A high-pressure system, in other words, can cause drought.

KEEPING THE PRESSURE ON

A few days of high air pressure aren't a bad thing. We all enjoy sunny days, when we can get outside and have fun. After a few days a high-pressure system usually moves on and is replaced by a low-pressure system. That's why a few sunny days are usually followed by a few days of rain or other precipitation. But sometimes a high-pressure system can become stalled. When this happens, a few dry, sunny days can stretch into several dry, sunny weeks. The result is a drought.

What can cause a high-pressure system to become stalled? There are several possibilities. They include powerful currents of air in the upper atmosphere and unusually warm or cold currents of water in the ocean.

Six miles above the surface of the earth blow some of the fastest winds known to scientists. They are called the *jet streams,* and

We all enjoy a chance to get outside
and have fun on warm, sunny days.

they blow in wide bands at speeds of up to 335 miles per hour. They get their name not only from their high speeds but because they were first discovered by jet airplanes just after World War II.

Although the jet streams are far above our heads, they can affect the weather here on the ground. Air-pressure systems that normally move around can become locked in place by the jet streams. A high-pressure system can become stalled in the same place for weeks or even months on end by the jet stream.

When this happens, the area underneath the high-pressure system can go for long periods without rain. If the high-pressure system is stalled long enough, the area can suffer a drought.

In the Pacific Ocean, along the equator, an unusual current of warm water appears every few years. It is known as *El Niño* (pronounced "el NEEN yo"), which is Spanish for "the boy." There is a similar current of cold water that appears from time to time known as *La Niña* ("lah NEEN ya"), or "the girl." (La Niña is also sometimes referred to as *El Viejo*—pronounced "ell vee AY ho"—or "the old man.") The two currents never appear at the same time.

Just as the jet streams can affect weather on the ground below, El Niño and La Niña can cause changes in the weather on nearby shores. In the United States, El Niño brings low-pressure areas, with hurricanes and other violent storms. La Niña, on the other hand, brings drought. In Asia, across the Pacific Ocean, the opposite is true. El Niño brings drought and La Niña brings storms.

Hurricane winds rip into the shore of a Florida beach resort community.

La Niña last appeared in 1988, bringing drought to the United States. Similarly, El Niño made its last major appearance in 1983, bringing severe drought to Australia, Indonesia, and even southern Africa.

Droughts can also occur simply because water doesn't get to the right place at the right time. Almost all of the water vapor in the air comes from the ocean, but not all of it falls back into the ocean as rain. Instead, the winds move the water-laden air onto dry land, where it becomes rain. In this way, water is moved from the ocean to areas where it is needed, such as the interiors of continents.

But the system doesn't always work correctly. Sometimes the winds that are needed to move the water-laden air inland are not strong enough. In the eastern United States, for instance, moist air is carried up from the south Atlantic and the Gulf of Mexico by winds blowing to the north. This air is then buffeted by other winds until it reaches the Great Plains states. The water carried by this air falls back to the ground as rain, nourishing the many farms in that region. In a year in which the winds don't blow at the right time or in the right direction, the moist air doesn't reach the Great Plains, and the area suffers from drought.

In Southeast Asia, the summer winds known as monsoons carry moist air from the Indian Ocean far inland. They provide rains that are badly needed after the dry winters in that region. Normally, the monsoon winds blow from south to north, but in some years they are blown to one side by winds from the west. When that happens, the moist air never leaves the Indian Ocean, and the rains don't reach the Asian continent. Many thousands of people can die as a result of the droughts that follow.

How the Great Plains Get Rain

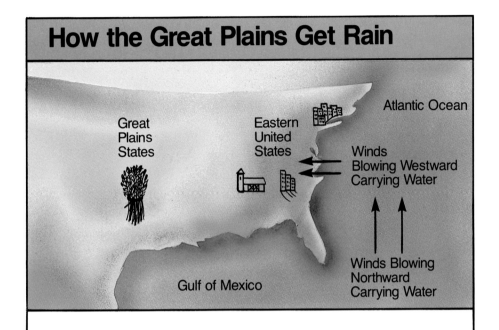

Great
Plains
States

Eastern
United
States

Atlantic Ocean

Winds
Blowing Westward
Carrying Water

Winds Blowing
Northward
Carrying Water

Gulf of Mexico

Moist air is carried north from the South Atlantic Ocean and the Gulf of Mexico. This air is then blown westward by winds blowing in from the ocean along the Atlantic coast. The air and water reaches the Great Plains states where it falls as rain.

Mountains can also prevent rain from reaching areas where it is needed. When air moves past a mountain, it is forced to rise in order to make it over the top. As it rises it gets colder, and the water vapor in the air turns back into liquid water. For that reason, rain tends to fall on the windward side of a mountain, the side that is

*A corn crop devastated
by drought.*

*In North Dakota, two scientists and a
farmer study the relationship between
drought and soil erosion.*

turned toward the wind. By the time the air gets over the mountain, most of the water vapor has been "squeezed" out of it. This is why many deserts, such as those in the American Southwest, are found on the opposite side of a mountain range from the ocean. In a sense, deserts are the result of a permanent drought.

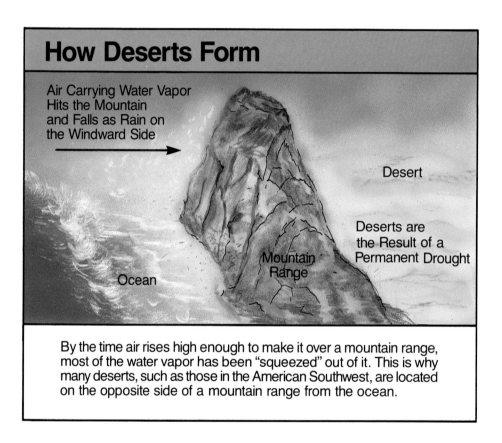

How Deserts Form

Air Carrying Water Vapor Hits the Mountain and Falls as Rain on the Windward Side

Desert

Deserts are the Result of a Permanent Drought

Mountain Range

Ocean

By the time air rises high enough to make it over a mountain range, most of the water vapor has been "squeezed" out of it. This is why many deserts, such as those in the American Southwest, are located on the opposite side of a mountain range from the ocean.

Deserts, such as Death Valley in California, are the result of a permanent drought.

PREHISTORIC DROUGHTS

The hydrologic cycle began a long time ago. The earth was born four and a half billion years ago out of hot, melted fragments in orbit around the sun. But at first the earth was too hot for water to exist in liquid form on its surface. Then the earth began to cool off. Rain began to fall. It fell steadily for millions of years, until the rain had literally filled the oceans.

It was in these oceans that the first life on earth formed. But lack of rain was not a problem for this early life. It had all the water it needed in the ocean itself. Then, about half a billion years ago, some fish were possibly caught in an ancient drought and adjusted to life on dry land for brief periods. (Alternately, they may have come on dry land to escape predators.) They passed this ability on to their offspring, who were also sometimes caught on dry land by drought. Eventually, some of these fish evolved into creatures who could live much of their life on dry land. And some of their offspring became creatures (like us) who live on dry land all the time. In a sense, we may live on dry land as the result of droughts that took place hundreds of millions of years ago.

These early dry-land creatures carried their own small ocean around with them, in the form of internal fluids. Even today, our bloodstream is a kind of miniature ocean that we take everywhere we go. But the price of living on dry land is that we must replenish our water supply from time to time or we will dry up. And drought can prevent us from replenishing that water.

There have been droughts ever since the first land creatures crawled out of the sea. We know this because we can see signs of these droughts, left over from ancient times. For instance, we can observe signs of droughts in ancient trees.

Dendrochronology is the science of studying tree rings. Tree rings are the dark bands that you see on the exposed surface of a tree stump when the tree is cut down. Every ring represents one year in the tree's growth. Some of the rings are wider than others. This tells us that the tree grew more in some years than in other years. Usually, the thinner tree rings occur in years of drought, when there is little water available to help the tree grow. Thus, these tree rings can tell us a lot about periods of drought in the past.

Trees can live for thousands of years. The oldest trees are nearly five thousand years old. And the fossilized remains of even older trees have been discovered by scientists.

Ancient tree rings studied in the southwestern United States tell us that this area underwent an unusually lengthy drought about two thousand years ago. Apparently the drought lasted for twenty-six years. Historians believe that it was responsible for a massive migration undertaken by the Pueblo Indians during this period.

Dendrochronology is the science of analyzing tree rings. Every ring represents one year—perhaps a dry one—in the tree's growth.

One of the most interesting things that scientists have discovered in studying tree rings is that droughts seem to come in cycles. In some areas, such as the western United States, the tree rings show that droughts occur approximately every twenty-two years. In others, such as China, they occur about every ten years.

Why should droughts occur in cycles? No one knows for sure, but a few scientists have pointed their fingers at *sunspots.*

Sunspots are dark, cool areas on the surface of the sun. (They are dark and cool compared with the rest of the surface of the sun, which is incredibly hot.) These spots appear and then disappear approximately every twenty-two years. At the beginning of the cycle, they start to appear. They grow in size and number until they

Sunspots are cool, dark areas on the surface of the sun. Some scientists have connected their appearances and disappearances to regular cycles of drought.

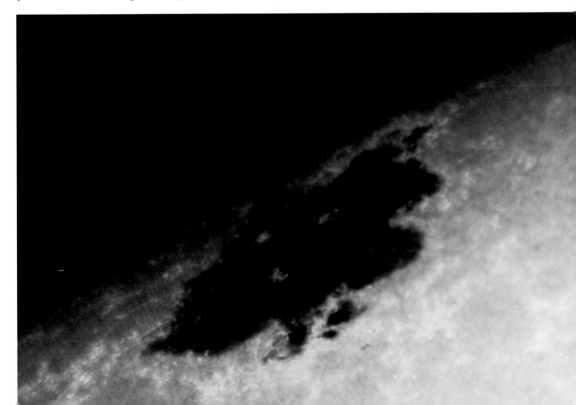

reach their maximum after eleven years. Then they dwindle away for the next eleven years, until the cycle begins again.

Sunspots are associated with streams of hot particles that are shot out from the sun and travel millions of miles through space. When these particles hit the earth's atmosphere—the shell of gases that surrounds our planet—they heat it up a little. The change in air temperature isn't enough to notice without special instruments, but a few scientists have suggested that it may be enough to affect our weather. And this, in turn, could cause droughts to occur at certain points in the sunspot cycle. Droughts in the American West do seem to occur on a twenty-two year cycle, just like sunspots.

There is much disagreement over this idea, however, and the number of scientists who believe in it are few. Still, it's an interesting idea to think about—that droughts on earth could be brought on by something happening 93 million miles away on the sun!

PREDICTING DROUGHTS

It would be nice if we could know in advance when a drought is on the way, so that we could be prepared for it. If the sunspot explanation is correct, for instance, then we could be safe in saying that droughts will appear at a certain point in the sunspot cycle. However, there is still no proof of the relationship between droughts and sunspots. And the sunspot explanation doesn't tell us just how severe the droughts are going to be.

We can, however, make predictions about the weather. And since it is the weather that causes droughts, we can use weather forecasts as a way of predicting droughts in advance.

Unfortunately, there is a limit to how far in advance the weather can be predicted. *Meteorologists*—scientists who study the weather— can make long-term weather forecasts, usually for a few months in

advance. But these forecasts are typically only about 60 percent accurate. (Forecasts made by flipping a coin are often 50 percent accurate.) Still, a 60 percent accurate forecast is better than nothing in the prediction of droughts.

Some scientists have even made longer-range predictions about the weather. These predictions indicate that there may be some severe droughts in our future. For many years, for instance, scientists noted that the global temperature—the average temperature of our planet over a one-year period—was decreasing. That is, the planet seemed to be growing colder. This global cooling trend, which began around the year 1950, showed that there would be shorter summers and very cold winters ahead. A few scientists even went so far as to suggest that we might be heading for another ice age, a period of thousands of years of below-average temperatures.

Colder temperatures usually bring high-pressure systems with them. And, as we saw earlier, high-pressure systems can cause drought. Thus, a period of lower temperatures could be a period of increased drought.

In recent years, however, this global cooling trend has begun to reverse itself. Temperatures have actually started going back up. Many scientists think that a global warming trend has begun.

Meteorologists try to make long-range predictions, as well as short-term forecasts. Their success rate, however, is not too impressive.

This Alaskan paper mill belching carbon dioxide into the air is contributing to the greenhouse effect, a global warming that may drastically affect our weather in the years to come.

What could be causing this global warming trend? Many scientists think that human beings are causing it. Certain gases produced by transportation systems and industrial activity, especially carbon dioxide, can cause too much heat from the sun to become trapped inside the earth's atmosphere, like heat in a greenhouse. For that reason, this is called a *greenhouse effect.* This trapped heat may gradually increase the global temperature, with disastrous results. The polar ice caps may begin to melt, raising the levels of the oceans and causing severe flooding along coastlines.

Ironically, this could also lead to drought. The increased temperatures could dry up water before it has a chance to nourish crops and other vegetation, resulting in dust bowls like the one in the 1930s.

Nobody knows if this is what will really take place. It is especially confusing because some scientists are predicting continued global cooling while others are predicting global warming. It's tempting to believe that the two trends will simply cancel one another out and that the global temperature will stay right where it is.

But the weather doesn't necessarily work that way. Meteorologists know that tiny changes in the way the weather works can often trigger larger changes in the weather. But these changes are difficult to predict in advance. Whatever the changes in our weather turn out to be, we can certainly hope that they don't lead to devastating droughts in our future!

GLOSSARY

air pressure—the force with which air presses down on the ground below.

barometer—a device for measuring air pressure.

barometric pressure—another term for air pressure.

black blizzard—a popular term for a dust storm.

climate—the weather pattern in a region over a long period of time.

condensation—the process by which water vapor turns into liquid water.

dendrochronology—the science of studying tree rings.

drought—a period when it rains less often than usual.

El Niño—an unusually warm current of water that appears periodically in the Pacific Ocean, along the equator.

El Viejo—another term for La Niña.

evaporation—the process by which liquid water turns into water vapor.

famine—a severe shortage of food, often brought on by drought.

greenhouse effect—the process by which the heat of the sun becomes trapped in our planet's atmosphere, raising the global temperature.

high-pressure system—an area in which the air pressure is high.

hydrologic cycle—the continuous process by which water evaporates and enters the air as water vapor, then falls back out as rain, only to evaporate again as water vapor.

jet streams—high-speed currents of air circling the world at heights of about 6 miles.

La Niña—an unusually cold current of water that appears periodically in the Pacific Ocean, near the equator.

low-pressure system—an area in which the air pressure is low.

meteorologists—scientists who study the weather.

monsoon—a wind that blows northward from the Indian Ocean toward the Asian continent, carrying moisture-laden air with it.

sunspots—dark, relatively cool areas on the surface of the sun.

water vapor—the invisible gaseous form of water.

RECOMMENDED READING

Bryson, Reid A. *Climates of Hunger.* Madison, Wis.: The University of Wisconsin Press, 1977.

Dolan, Edward F. *Drought: The Past, Present and Future Enemy.* New York: Franklin Watts, 1990.

Fradin, Dennis Brindell. *Droughts.* Chicago: Childrens Press, 1983.

INDEX

ABOUT THE AUTHOR

Christopher Lampton is a free-lance writer. Born in Brownsville, Texas, he has a bachelor of arts degree in radio, TV, and film from the University of Maryland.

Mr. Lampton has more than fifty non-fiction science books to his credit and nine works of fiction, including several science fiction novels for Doubleday and Laser Books. He currently lives outside Washington, D.C.